UMBRIA

TREADING THE PATH OF ART AND SOUL

WHITE STAR
PUBLISHERS

CONTENTS

Introduction Page 12

A green oasis of peace Page 18

Art RULES supreme Page 42

The mysticism of Nature Page 128

Text
Maria Laura della Croce

Photographs
Giulio Veggi

Editorial Supervision
Valeria Manferto

Editorial coordination
Laura Accomazzo

Graphics
Patrizia Balocco
Anna Galliani

Translation
Jane Glover

© 1995 White Star S.r.l.
Via C. Sassone, 22/24
13100 Vercelli
www.whitestar.it

ISBN 88-8095-172-6

Reprints:
2 3 4 5 6   06 05 04 03 02

Printed in Italy

1 Close-up of the façade of the Cathedral of Norcia showing the statue of Saint Benedict.

2-3 The ancient fortified town of Trevi with its steep slopes and characteristic medieval and Renaissance dwellings.

4-5 The Carceri Hermitage lies on the wooded slopes of Mt. Subasio, two and a half miles from Assisi, immersed in a dense forest of holly oaks. Silence bathes the cloister, the oratory, the Chapel of St. Mary, and the chancel, all built in miniature proportions. This is where Saint Francis liked to retreat to pray.

6-7 The Sybilline Mountains are the "upper" part of Umbria. The tallest peak is Mt. Vettore, almost 8,200 feet above sea level. These are "unquiet" mountains, featuring frequent seismic activity and karstic formations. They are known for their huge underground systems of caves and tunnels and for the many rare species of animals they harbor.

8-9 The fifteenth-century painters were masters at creating works which captured the delicate serenity of the Umbrian landscape perfectly, with its characteristic gentle slopes and harmonious colors.

10-11 The traditional Festival of the Ceri at Gubbio is held annually on May 15, the feast day of Saint Ubaldo, the city's patron saint.

INTRODUCTION

Umbria is the only region in central Italy without any coastline. It is equidistant from the Adriatic and Tyrrhenian Seas as well as from Lombardy and Calabria. This isolation distinguishes it from the rest of Italy and lies at the heart of both its strengths and its limitations.

Umbria is a mountainous region, packed tight with crags, cliffs, and ridges, criss-crossed with tortuous, inaccessible roads, punctuated by castles, watchtowers, and huge defensive walls built high to shelter the houses, and scattered throughout with dense, dark, oak trees. But impermeability and

isolation, which characterize this area with its fortified towns and villages, built to withstand the brutality and violence which have marked its past, are what make the Umbria of today so fascinating and powerfully evocative. Its unique historical and geographical background has preserved it more than other regions from the modern process of savage urbanization, just as in more distant times it preserved it from large settlements and change. If Umbria is still in some ways a farming community, a silent and archaic place still preserving human proportions which, time after time, enchant visitors, these barriers are to thank. Even its colors are unchanging: the pale stone of Assisi known as pietra serena or serene stone, the brick-red of Todi, the yellow tufa of Orvieto, and the dull, ash-grey stone of Gubbio.

Umbria's ancient nature is particularly suited to the adjectives most often used to describe it such as green, mystical, and Franciscan. However, there is a strongly contrasting side, too. The sweet, idyllic panorama which the Umbrian painters of the fifteenth century portrayed with such grace could on occasions be harsh and even hostile. Landscapes whose perfect harmony had the power to move the soul were depicted alongside others so horrid and solemn as to arouse fear and awe. Likewise, a spiritual, silent Umbria, can be found in its abbeys and its convents, and in St. Francis's "Canticle of the Sun" and Jacopone of Todi's "Lauds," alongside its joyous, lively counterpart found in the narrow streets, the shops, the village festivals, or sitting at table amidst roast piglet, truffles, and full-bodied wines. Giotto, seven hundred years ago, distanced himself from the contemplative Franciscan myth and painted at Assisi the story of an energetic, volatile saint, a man who knew his own stature and his own strengths, a new man, enterprising and active.

12 Perched on the top of a hill, the village of Trevi looks down on the Spoleto valley.

13 The façade of the Duomo of Orvieto, richly decorated with sculpture and painting.

14-15 The interior of the Upper Church of St. Francis at Assisi is decorated with works by Cimabue and his pupils and by Giotto's cycle of 28 frescoes.

16-17 The warm colors of the setting sun seem to embrace the quilted rooftops of Perugia, clad in the characteristic local terracotta pantiles.

18-19 Even in the middle of the country, as in this photograph of Todi, there are valuable palaces and impregnable fortresses, testifying to the ancient pomp and power of this historic part of Italy.

A GREEN OASIS OF PEACE

20 top Horses graze in an olive grove near Ferentillo.

20 center Gently rolling hills, rows of cypresses, and ancient buildings are typical of the landscape around Spello.

20 bottom Olive trees have always been a constant presence in Umbria.

21 The spectacular leaps of the Marmore Falls, 541 feet high, burst into the green of the Umbrian countryside. The falls were created by Curius Dentatus in 273 B.C. when, in order to prevent the river Velino from flooding the surrounding area, he diverted its course into the nearby river Nera.

Throughout central Italy the hills have always been deemed the most favorable place to live and the most human environment. For centuries the plain represented a hostile site for human settlement because of the perils of marshland, malaria, and military invasion, whereas the mountains were a shelter in times of war and other troubles, relegated to the perimeter of life due to their height and steep slopes, their harsh climate, isolation, and their lack of adequate means of communications. Almost half of Umbria consists of hill country, the contours making gentle outlines, easy slopes, and modest altitudes. Man's imprint here became progressively more marked as the roads and settlements increased. This is where cities like Orvieto, Perugia, Assisi, and Norcia were established and able to grow.

In Umbria even the land was well-prepared for war, almost as if it had been designed for defense. Even farmhouses partook of this state of mind and were often built well away from roads, out of an instinctive diffidence towards passers-by. The characteristic tower-shaped columbariums which punctuate the valleys and the plains are like sentinels or keeps. Many fortified towns and villages were built on top of mountains or practically inaccessible hillsides such as Campello Alto, Trevi, Spello, Corciano, Cerreto, Montescuto, and Scoppio. These last few are true mountain towns, wild places, when not openly hostile, more similar to the Meteora and Mt. Athos of Greece than to the gentle hills depicted by Perugino.

Then there are the fortresses, the bastions, the narrow streets, and the towers found all over the region. From Assisi to Spoleto, from Perugia to Narni, they present a variegated set of landscapes in which the presence of the old abbeys is a dominant one. The buttresses of the Holy Convent of Assisi hurled their challenge at the enemy as he advanced from the other end of the valley. The ancient abbey of Magione, home to the Knights Templar, whose order aroused fear in Pope and Emperor alike, had its walls reinforced, barricaded, and equipped like a castle, fortified with a look-out and defense towers, until over the course of the centuries it was transformed into one of the most impressive examples of military architecture in the region.

22-23 Delicate willow trees bend gently and are mirrored in the clear waters of Clitumnus. The romantic setting of this famous spring has inspired artists and poets throughout history.

24-25 Faroaldo II, Duke of Spoleto, had the ancient abbey of St. Peter's in the Valley built in the valley of the Nera, at the foot of Mount Solenne, in the eighth century. The imposing architectural complex from the Dark Ages is a rich source of knowledge about pictorial art in the years between the Byzantine and Romanesque periods.

26 top Lake Piediluco, which the ancient Romans called Lacus Velinus, with its surrounding woodland, is one of the most enchanting and romantic landscapes in the whole of Umbria. Much visited by nature lovers, the lake is also used for world-class rowing competitions.

26 center Lake Corbara has its own unique appeal even though it is not a natural lake.

26 bottom Lake Trasimeno, one of the largest Italian lakes, is famous for its rich fishing. In fact, the three islands which emerge from the lake are inhabited by fishermen.

This is where, in 1502, they organized the plot against Caesar Borgia, known as Il Valentino. The whole of Umbria is sprinkled with abbey fortresses. Some still living, some in ruins, they leave a characteristic footprint on the landscape. As the rulers of large estates they played an important role in reclaiming the territory and were landmarks in a landscape in the process of being defined. The classical, traditional view of Umbria is, therefore, of a "castled" land bristling with fortresses. There must have been plenty of them too, if a census taken at the end of the eighteenth Century counted more than 140 around Perugia alone.

But the Umbrian scenery is just as famous for its country roads, winding through hillsides, plateaus, forests, vineyards, and olive groves. Sometimes enclosed within the circle of the city walls, the olive groves of Assisi, Spello, Spoleto, Foligno, and Trevi used to supply the Roman court, the Marches, and even Romagna. They alternate now with the long, low rows of vines, creating an enchanting atmosphere which persists even today, despite the region's progressive industrialization. The best way to travel Umbria is to leave the car at home and use a motorcycle, a bicycle or, best of all, a horse, and succumb to the temptation of the past and of a slower pace of life. In this way one can best enjoy the silence and the "green heart of Italy," where art and nature seem almost to have purposely combined their energies to stage this spectacle. There is a tremendous choice of countryside itineraries. This description by Montaigne, who was thrilled by a journey he took through Umbria in 1581, gives some idea of the variety of scenery on offer, such as in the valley around Foligno where there are "…a thousand different hills covered everywhere with every species of fruit tree, the most beautiful valleys, an infinite number of streams, not an inch of useless land…and among mountains as fertile as these, can be seen the Apennines showing their inaccessible, almost scowling peaks, from which flow torrents that will shortly become gentle, pleasing brooks."

27 The richness of the Umbrian countryside is due partly to the amount of fresh water within its borders that contain several lakes. In the photograph, Lake Piediluco is a deep, chill stretch of water, yet a very romantic one.

28-29 The sun's rays have penetrated the late morning mist to light up the village of Corbara, but the white cloak still conceals the slopes on which the old town sits and hides the eponymous artificial lake in its embrace.

The Sybilline Mountains, in the heart of the central Apennines, offer another kind of scenario, rich in deep valleys, dwindling into fearsome narrow gorges through which burst tumultuous rivers. It is not surprising that the Medieval literature which grew out of the local legends placed the home of Virgil's soothsayer on Mt. Sybil, "at the entrance to Hell." Castelluccio, the highest and most picturesque of the districts of Norcia and famous for its small, sweet lentils which grow at the foot of the town, sits here on its rocky spur, among mountains where the Apennine wolf still lives and golden eagles nest. The karstic mountains around Castelluccio are only accessible on foot along ancient footpaths and mule tracks. The crisp air, the solitude, the ruined castles and towers, the meadows and woodland, sink-holes, and a superb view of the plains stretching out at the foot of the snowy peaks all contribute towards making this one of the most imposing settings of the entire Apennine chain. Valnerina, the valley of the river Nera between Spoleto and Norcia, is another area of particular natural and ecological interest. The landscape goes from precipices and tunnels gouged through the rock to thick forests of chestnut trees, box oaks, and juniper trees.

30 left The unmistakable character of the Umbria panorama can be identified in its extraordinary variety of colors and landscapes. This photograph captures the delicate harmony of the many different blossoms seen on the Grand Plain of Castelluccio di Norcia.

30-31 and 31 bottom At 3,937 feet above sea level, the views from the Grand Plain of Castelluccio di Norcia are stunning. It is a tapestry of colors: the vibrant hues of the tulips, the bright yellow of the buttercups, the vermilion of the poppies, the emerald green of the meadows, and the gold of the corn.

32-33 *The spectacular "flowering" of the plain which lies in front of Castelluccio di Norcia, the only town at the foot of the Sybilline Mountains, situated at 4,757 feet above sea level.*

Down below flow the transparent waters of the river Nera and mirrored in the water is Vallo di Nera, one of the best-preserved of the Umbrian walled villages, the pattern of its streets still a faithful mirror of the fourteenth-century layout. It is like going back in time: cars are rare, lonely churches alternate with crenellated walls, roads and rivers run superimposed upon each another, with grey and yellow limestone rocks as a backdrop to the dark green of the dense vegetation.

"When the air is still, the sound of the waterfall can be heard a long way away. The cascade is formed by the waters of the Velino. From its course over scattered rocks it plunges suddenly downward as the ground falls away under it, falling into a stone basin and bouncing spectacularly up. From the basin it falls in jets onto three spurs of rock which dam its fall. Leaping over in three wheels of seething water it falls into a second basin from whence, to the accompaniment of a great noise, it hurls itself into the bed of the Nera, which is so shocked by this unexpected slap that it takes a while to recover from the surprise and the excitement." This was how the scholarly French archeologist and eighteenth-century traveller Charles de Brosses, described his reaction to another of the spectacular sights of Umbria - the Marmore waterfall, later immortalized in Byron's poetry. Although a stunning phenomenon, it is not wholly natural. The Romans created the waterfall as part of the reclamation of the marshes on the plains of Rieti.

34-35 Numerous flocks of sheep graze on the slopes of the Sybilline Mountains from May onwards. The pastures are very abundant and can feed tens of thousands of sheep through to late September.

36-37 The fertile clods of newly-ploughed soil reveal the wealth of the Umbrian earth. This large field is part of the countrystde surrounding the ancient town of Todi. Perhaps this kind of idyllic rural setting makes it easier to approach "the places of the spirit," with greater awareness and serenity.

The Romans also conditioned the Umbrian countryside around Lake Trasimeno, which is shallow and has no natural outlets. In the first century A.D. the Emperor Claudius had a drain built to regulate floods and stabilize the water level. The fourth largest Italian lake in surface area, Trasimeno is gentle, ruffled with wavelets, its shores mantled with olive groves and vineyards which alternate with dense Mediterranean scrubland. Three small islands rise in the lake, their dark green stains breaking the clear blue of the lake waters.

38-39 Two typical facets of the Umbrian character -- order and precision -- are reflected in the countryside around Todi.

40-41 A clean blue sky streaked with pure white clouds overlooks a tobacco plantation.

42-43 An unusual photograph taken at Assisi after a heavy snowfall, with the façade of the Church of St. Francis emerging like a ghost from the mist.

ART RULES
SUPREME

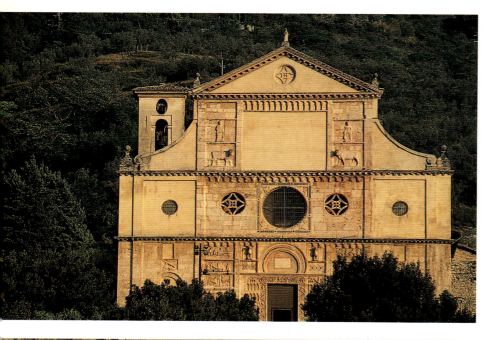

Umbria is as memorable for its artistic heritage as it is for the delights of its countryside. It might seem that as far as art is concerned, its proximity to Tuscany and the inevitable comparisons might prove disadvantageous for the smaller, out-of-the-way, more provincial region, but it is not so. Firstly, for centuries Umbria has been a compulsory stage in the itinerary of European travelers and scholars as they journeyed from Venice and Florence to Rome and Naples. Secondly, the quantity and the truly exceptional quality of the artistic masterpieces, for the most part in an excellent state of preservation and distributed over a relatively small area, justifies the artistic importance of a region which is very popular with foreign visitors, increasing numbers of whom are choosing the towns and villages of Umbria for their holidays or even for their permanent homes. The oldest known history of Umbria goes back to the Etruscans, who settled mainly in areas to the east of the Tiber River. The artistic and social achievements of this civilization are demonstrated by the remains which have survived until our times: the impressive Etruscan arch in Perugia, the Tomb of the Volumnii with its poignant sarcophagi, and the Eugubine Tablets inscribed with the symbols and allusions of that esoteric world. Roman Umbria has left behind wonderful architectural remains and urban sites, too: the Temple of Minerva at Assisi, the theaters and amphitheaters at Gubbio, Spoleto, Bevagna, and Todi, the walls and bridges at Perugia, Narni and Foligno, and a city like Carsulae, its structures entire and intact since Augustan times. But there is no doubt that the most strongly representative face of Umbria is the one left by the epoch of the free, independent commonwealths which thrived during the passage from the Romanesque to the Gothic period. It is almost impossible to count the churches, the chapels, the abbeys, the monasteries, the sanctuaries, and the mountain hermitages, culminating in the Duomo of Orvieto, San Rufino at Assisi, Spoleto, or San Lorenzo at Perugia. Their richly adorned interiors are the material manifestation of mysticism and prayer.

At the same time, the civil and military

44-45 Spoleto, St. Peter's Outside the Walls. The richly carved façade of the church, set at the gates of Spoleto, is considered one of the greatest masterpieces of Romanesque sculpture in Umbria. Divided into three horizontal sections, the lowest tier has three portals flanked by lively illustrations of Biblical scenes and animal figures. The exquisite execution and naturalness of the carvings, which date from the beginning of the thirteenth century, indicate that Benedetto Antelami may have been their creator.

46-47 Founded around 1000, the Benedictine Abbey of Sassovivo lies in a wonderful setting near Foligno.

architecture gives the whole region its characteristically defensive look, a clear indication of the long and hard-fought Middle Ages. Perugia fought against Assisi and Foligno, Foligno fought against Spoleto, Terni against Narni, and so on. Hostilities did not just have territorial bases, but political ones too. Perugia, for example, was a Guelphic stronghold while Foligno was held by the Ghibellines. Thus fortresses, castles, towered palaces, walls, and complex defensive sites occupied the hills, completed the villages, and redesigned the cities.

During the exile of the popes to Avignon in the 14th Century, Innocent VI tried to re-annex the Umbrian cities to the Papal State, entrusting the task to a Spaniard, Cardinal Albornoz. Under Albornoz, Umbria lived its golden period of constructive fervor, with Papal fortifications erected at Spoleto, Assisi, and Narni. The fortresses, symbols of the reaffirmation of the Church's temporal power and important links in the communications between Rome and its territories in the Marches and Romagna, were joined by public palaces representing local power: the Palace of the People at Todi, the Palace of the Captain at Orvieto, of the Priors at Perugia, and of the Consuls at Gubbio. They expressed both formidable engineering and building techniques and vast, new, artistic intuition, as well as representing communal society in its entirety. Georges Duby says that "The people of Gubbio closed their consuls within a marvelous fortress and at enormous cost built next to it a huge open terrace not dedicated to trade. On this stage they performed their civic rites, beneath the Umbrian sky." The crenellated walls and, sometimes, watchtowers, lived on in memory of the ancient defensive function, but town palaces were opening up towards the outside. With the addition of porticos on the ground floors, double and triple mullioned windows on the higher floors, balconies, and wide external stairways the militaristic look of the fortresses gradually began to disappear and the large, single, first-floor rooms were ideal for rich decorations, such as frescoes. Such rigorous and elegant architecture ended up becoming the most natural site for the innumerable artists and sculptors who contributed towards creating those

46 bottom and 47 right The celebrated Romanesque cloister is the work of the Roman stone mason Pietro De Maria. Each piece, including the 128 pillars, *the arches, and the entablature, was carved at Rome and transported along the Tiber to Orte, from where it was transported overland to Sassovivo.*

"total works of art" which are so widespread throughout Umbria.

In cathedrals and in patrician palaces alike, there were painters, sculptors, mosaicists, marble masons, stone-carvers, decorators, inlayers, engravers, and miniaturists working alongside the architects, the master stonecutters, the masons, and the builders. Although true for many men of the era, in particular Oderisi da Gubbio was immortalized by Dante in The Inferno when he wrote, "Oh! -- I said to him -- are you not Oderisi, honored of Gubbio and honored of that art which in Paris is called illumination?." They came from far and wide, each bringing a unique sum of skills and culture, in function of the widely differing requirements of their patrons. The mobility of artists and craftsmen had been common for a long time, and to this was added the intertwining of patrician family ties, movements within the Church, captains on missions, and teachers and students moving between places of study. An idea of the wealth of stimuli and the cultural traffic which Umbria was already witnessing in the second half of the thirteenth century can be grasped by the fact that the first decorations of the Upper Church at Assisi were done by French and English frescoists and master glaziers.

The painting of the walls of the two basilicas was shared by the Florentines Cimabue and, in several different stages, Giotto, as well as Roman, Sienese, and some Umbrian artists. Meanwhile the Sacred Convent was being enriched by French miniatures, fabrics from Palermo, and Venetian gold and silver. At Perugia the great Pisan sculptors decorated Piazza Maggiore with its famous fountain and the Sienese were in charge of work on the great site of the Orvieto cathedral, where artists of the caliber of Arnolfo di Cambio worked.

A formidable trio of sculptors, Nicola Pisano, his son Giovanni, and their pupil, Arnolfo di Cambio, worked in Umbria throughout the second half of the thirteenth century, producing a series of masterpieces which marked the affirmation of a "national" artistic language. Together they set up a flourishing workshop which revealed uncommon entrepreneurial talents, becoming famous on a European scale. The two Pisanos are credited with the fountain in Piazza Maggiore in Perugia, the oldest public fountain in Italy and the first political monument linked to civil power.

The words of praise inscribed on the marble basin give some idea of the artists' self-esteem and the consideration in which they were held, "These are the names of the excellent sculptors of the fountain: Nicola, famous in this art, appreciated for all his works, flower among sculptors and most agreeable among the good; parent is the first, dearest of sons the second, whom if you do not wish to be mistaken, you will call Giovanni. Pisans by birth, may they long enjoy good health ...." The fountain's complex sculptural decoration is the first example of an encyclopedic-allegorical plan, with religious themes mixed with political symbols and exhortations about civic ethics. Arnolfo di Cambio, a celebrated architect as well as a sculptor, was also responsible in Umbria for the funereal monument to French Cardinal de Braye in the church of San Domenico in Orvieto. It is a complex work of sculpture and architecture, enriched with colored areas of mosaic and inlay. The figure of the cardinal, lying on top of the sarcophagus, cruelly underlines the advanced age of the dead man and reveals Arnolfo's interest in detailed and realistic analysis as applied to portraiture. Almost fifty years after the wonders which issued from the workshop of the Pisanos, another great artist, Lorenzo Maitani, was nominated master builder of the Duomo of Orvieto. His façade drew its inspiration from Siena's cathedral and he was responsible for the noblest of the carvings on the buttresses flanking the portals, illustrating the stories of Genesis and the Last Judgment. Rows of the damned are grasped by terrible devils from Hell, in a tumult extraordinary enough to capture the notice of Pope Pius II Piccolomini, whose Commentaries were later to contain words of praise for the sculptor.

However, it is the paintings of Umbria which truly deserve the description "triumphant." There are at least four cities very important to the art of painting: Assisi, first of all, thanks to the extraordinary Franciscan epic, Perugia with the impetuous growth of the municipality's political and economic role, and lastly, Spoleto and Orvieto. At

49 Sweetness and greatness emanate from the splended Annunciation painted by Perugino's pupil Pinturicchio in 1501. It is part of the cycle of frescoes depicting the life of the Virgin Mary in the Baglioni Chapel of St. Mary Major at Spello. The self-portrait on the right of the picture underlines the importance the artist attributed to this work.

Assisi there are the spectacular cycles of frescoes by Giotto and his helpers. The stories of the Old Testament and of St. Francis are interpreted in the Upper Church, the story of the Maddalena is rendered in the chapel which bears her name, and the Childhood of Christ is depicted in the Lower Church. These works were completed in the last years of the thirteenth century, a surprisingly precocious date for this series of innovative works and their contents. Critics have mentioned pre-Humanism, anthropocentrism *ante litteram*, *and studies in perspective and space which were revolutionary for the times. Scenes which were conventionally treated in a courtly, symbolic style were suffused by Giotto with humanity, emotions, and reality; the aftershock caused by his work was limitless. Thus, from the turn of the thirteenth Century, one can already talk of the Umbrian Giotto factor, in which the great Franciscan cycle had become the new linguistic foundation, revealing strong, independent personalities as it was progressively interpreted. The factor's extremely wide diffusion, centered in Umbria because of the magnetic pole of attraction at Assisi, was ground for its diverse expression in the region's most vital towns where original interpretations of these models were produced. Both Orvieto and Perugia, for example, opened up to the lively, contemporary Sienese culture, employing its best artists, from Simone Martini to Lorenzo Maitani to the cathedral choirmaster. There was also an important link with the school of international Gothic art, the point of reference for the anonymous Umbrian masters who decorated the Trinci Palace at Foligno at the beginning of the fifteenth century. The residence of the town's overlords is frescoed with a series of illustrious men of gigantic proportions and, in the Chamber of Stars, with portrayals of the liberal arts, the planets, and the ages of man. Nowadays, the cycle is considered the most varied work of fifteenth-century secular art in central Italy, portraying a sort of encyclopedia of contemporary Humanist culture. During this same early fifteenth-century period, the greatest artists to be found in Italy were working in Perugia and nearby, including Domenico Veneziano, Beato Angelico, Filippo Lippi,*

50 Built over a period of time from the twelfth to the fifteenth centuries, the Palace of the Priors superbly expresses the spirit of communal Perugia. The square dressed stone, broken only by two rows of Gothic triple-mullioned windows, gives the building the severe, shuttered look of a tall, powerful bastion.

51 One of the two stone griffins standing guard on either side of the superb doorway of the Palace of the Priors on Corso Vannucci. This mythical animal is Perugia's emblem.

52-53 A panoramic view of the ancient town of Cascia. Birthplace of St. Rita and one of the most important centers of pilgrimage in Italy, Cascia has ancient origins. It was a Roman town and then an important ecclesiastical center in the Middle Ages.

Piero della Francesca, and Benozzo Bozzoli. The latter, a pupil of Beato Angelico and famous for his work for the Medici, produced his first large commission in Montefalco, a cycle of frescoes depicting the life of St. Francis in the saint's ex-Church, now an art gallery.

Perugia proudly guarded its own identity and it was, not surprisingly, the last of the cities to allow itself to be assimilated by the Papal States. It was within this context that at the end of the fifteenth century an art style developed which was unique to the town and which gained international fame. It was a style which idealized both figures and landscape, joining them in a pattern of simple and at the same time extremely precise, studied lines, filling them with a diffused, high, serene light. This is the eponymous Umbrian art, the "fifteenth-century Perugia" which is seen at its very best in the Perugino frescoes at the Collegio del Cambio (Exchange Guild). The success of this art grew and diversified as it was applied to the decorative arts of stone inlay, marquetry, woven fabrics, and the majolica ware of Deruta. Pietro Vannucci, called Perugino, was the region's greatest artist. He lived in the fourteenth and fifteenth centuries and headed one of the most prolific and celebrated workshops of

53 Terni is a modern, sometimes avant-garde, industrial city, but its roots go back a long way into the past. Remains testifying to the historical importance of this provincial capital include precious Romanesque churches and sumptuous sixteenth- and seventeenth-century palaces, like those in the photograph.

the Italian Renaissance. He invented a style which fused the quality of Piero della Francesca's treatment of light with the soft lines of Verrocchio's art. Since the first manifestation of the new Perugian art, the Miracles of St. Bernadine, by way of the celebrated Madonnas spread throughout half the museums in Europe, and through his work in Rome including the Handing over of the Keys in the Sistine Chapel, right up to the frescoes in the Collegio del Cambio at Perugia where he had in the meantime been made an honorary citizen,

Perugino's ability to create these new images is manifest, transmitting a sweet sentiment of holiness and asceticism in a balanced union of virtue, order, and equilibrium. His expressive style was immediately recognized and appreciated by his contemporaries and was, of course, the starting point from which the sublime art of Raffaello Sanzio later developed. Luca Signorelli was another great Umbrian artist of the period. His painting of the Martyrdom of St. Sebastian is preserved in the Città di Castello art gallery, his altarpiece of the same name, with its magnificent portrayal in the foreground of the angel musician intent on tuning his instrument, is at Perugia and, most important of all, Orvieto has his frescoes in the Chapel of St. Brizio in the Duomo, unanimously considered to be his greatest masterpiece. Unlike the contemplative, peaceful aura which shines from the work of Perugino, Signorelli's frescoes of Hell at Orvieto with the stories of the Antichrist and the Apocalypse have figures multiplying at a wild rhythm, forming increasingly complex and dynamic compositions, until they seem about to break out of their frames. Some critics have seen a definite precursor for the painting of Michelangelo in the plasticity and energy of Signorelli's bodies. Others, like Argan, saw "a grandiose, spectacular, extremely effective representation, intended beyond any doubt to terrify the faithful, to persuade them to believe in the true prophecies, and to reject what is false. Perugino soothes, Signorelli shocks. Perhaps the cause of the greater intensity of his painting is the imminence of religious strife. Shock is a stronger, more topical argument than contemplation." Perhaps it is the Franciscan aura, or the rural archaisms, or the sight of nature in its uncontaminated state. Whatever the reason, Umbria, more than any other of the Italian regions, allows us to rediscover the silent interior dimension which many have forgotten, used as they are to the frenzied, mechanical rhythms of their contemporary lifestyles.

The enchantment of the Umbrian towns lies in the sound of our footsteps on the unchanged streets of ancient settlements, in the sense of time which emanates from every detail, in the emotions awoken by a lonely spire against a backdrop of farmland, a convent with its kitchen produce and its formal garden, the orderly alternation of colors in the natural landscape, the yellow of its clay, and the grey of the Medieval buildings. Although it is true that Umbria in its entirety is a kind of open-air museum, since even the tiny villages teetering on the crests of mountains and hilltops are saturated with ancient history, it is also true that some towns preserve so much of the past as to make them uniquely fascinating. Città di Castello lies almost on the Tuscan border. Beloved of Pliny who had a villa there, its ruling families were friends of the Medici and they summoned Florentine architects like Antonio da Sangallo and Giorgio Vasari to build their dwellings, decorating them later with works by the most successful artists of the period, from Raphael who painted his famous Marriage of the Virgin here, to Della Robbia, and from Signorelli to Rosso Fiorentino. Gubbio, which dominates the plain surrounding it, is protected by wooded mountains and limestone cliffs. Its unique position on the slopes makes a magnificent sight even from a distance, with the most important of its buildings -- the Palace of the Consuls, the Duomo, and the Church of St. John -- clearly visible. The town has hardly changed since the fifteenth century. Miraculously, its proud, austere, Medieval mould has been preserved up to our times, in part thanks to the hardness of the limestone rock traditionally used in Gubbian architecture. At the beginning of this century, Hermann Hesse was an enthusiastic, stunned, visitor here and he left a vivid description of the town. He wrote of the Palace of Consuls that, "the grandiose, almost reckless audacity of this architecture produces an absolutely staggering effect and it has something which is both unreal and perturbing about it. It is like a dream, or coming face to face with a theatrical setting. You have constantly to remind yourself that this is not the case, but that it is really there, unmoving, fixed in stone. There is something mythical, almost primordial, in the boldness which built on this steep hill and challenged unusual obstacles, which raised dizzying towers and colossal fortresses on a handkerchief of earth and then put monasteries and massive castles on the peak, along the crest of the craggy rock."

55 Luca Signorelli's altarpiece of the martyrdom of St. Sebastian depicts him standing against a sky full of ruins, his tormentors portrayed with elegant angularity, whirling around him, in a dance of death. The work dates from 1496 and is in the Città di Castello Art Gallery.

Every year, halfway through May, Gubbio's mysticism is thrust into the foreground with the Feast of the Ceri in honor of St. Ubaldo, the city's patron saint. Three hundred Ceraioli have the task of bearing the three wooden ceri, or church candles (each of which weighs over 1,000 pounds), in a frenzied two-and-a-half-mile race around the town. The Elevation of the Ceri is one of the oldest ceremonies in Italy, going back to the thirteenth century, and one of the most popular. To say that Perugia is a city with a thousand faces is practically to state the obvious. The settlements which have succeeded each other over the centuries are documented by a series of masterpieces which have been miraculously preserved until our time. Thus, we have the powerful Etruscan city walls, the gates, the arch, and the Tomb of the Volumnii; the old city with the most beautiful medieval fountain in Italy; the austere Palace of the Priors; and inside, that most extraordinary of the monuments of Renaissance art, the Collegio del Cambio, with frescoes by Perugino. However, the landscape, green and hilly, just a short way from Lake Trasimeno, the Umbrian "sea," with its birds and fish, is still triumphant over all these wonders of human art and artifice. In his travels through Italy at the end of the eighteenth century, Goethe related that the "city is set in a beautiful position, the view of the lake delightful; I impressed these visions upon my memory." The city of St. Francis is so linked to the name of its most illustrious citizen that a mystical, luminous aura seems to emanate from it. The gentle, serene valley in which it lies contributes to this aura, as it stretches along a line from Perugia to Spoleto to form an arc 25 miles long. Assisi and the area around it is the appropriate place to encounter St. Francis. It is possible to visit the house where he was born, the Duomo where he was baptized, the Archbishop's Palace where he rejected his father's authority, and St. Damian where Christ asked him to rebuild the ruined church. But Assisi is also the center of the Umbrian valley, the same one which appears in the background of landscapes by Perugino or in early Raphaels, harmonious, reassuring, perfect, a landscape which seems to have been transfigured by grace or by enchantment.

58-59 *The door-jamb of the central portal of the church of St. Michael in Bevagna, thought to date from the twelfth Century, bears the figure of the Archangel Michael.*

"I have seen nothing more serene," said St. Francis himself, when describing his valley. "Nothing can equal it," said Hyppolite Taine and, "before seeing Assisi one can have no idea of the art or of the genius of the Middle Ages. Add Dante and the **Little Flowers** of St. Francis and you have the masterpiece of mystical Christianity."

Foligno is one of the rare Umbrian towns to have grown up on the plain on a site favorable to communication, which allowed it to become a flourishing commercial center ever since Roman times as well as to acquire an important cultural and artistic heritage. As early as midway through the fifteenth century the art of printing was flourishing in Foligno. The first edition of The "Divine Comedy" was published in the town in 1472, the first book in Italian to be printed in Italy. Foligno also preserves what is perhaps the most varied example of secular decoration from fifteenth-century central Italy in the Trinci Palace, where the lords of the city lived.

The countryside around Foligno, with its "many rich plains stretching as far as the eye can see," impressed a sophisticated traveler like Montaigne who, however upset by the fact that "they do not cook artichokes (sic!), they serve marinated fish, for they have none of the fresh variety, and they serve raw broad beans, peas, and green almonds" did admit "it does seem to me that no painter could depict such a rich countryside." Curiously, Goethe, two centuries later, also recalled about the town's alimentary habits that, "here in Foligno, in a house furnished in pure Homeric style, everyone sits in a huge room around a fire lit in the bare earth, shouting and carrying on while eating at a long table like the one in pictures of the Wedding of Cana."

For a long time the Trinci of Foligno were also the lords of Bevagna, a minor city and one which lies remote and out of time, whose particular attraction lies in the silence and austerity of Piazza Silvestri, its asymmetrical, Romanesque heart.

"Although boldly built and looking like a proud, bellicose fortress, nowadays Montefalco is one of the most peace-loving places on earth, a tranquil center of Franciscan art. Wherever you look,

59 Piazza Silvestri in Bevagna, with its irregular shape and its flagstones echoing with the footsteps of inhabitants and visitors alike, is one of the most beautiful squares in central Italy. Round it stand the churches of St. Michael and of St. Sylvester, jewels of Romanesque architecture, and the Gothic-style Palace of the Consuls. At its center stands a splendidly decorative Romanesque fountain.

60 top The Porziuncola is situated underneath the cupola of the huge Church of St. Mary of the Angels, the seventh biggest in the

Christian world, built in Assisi in the late sixteenth century to hold the enormous crowds of pilgrims.

wherever you walk, everything is ancient, medieval, stony, cold, and hard. Tiny lanes cut through tall houses of undressed stone, ancient towers, gateways, castles, churches, and walls." This is how Hesse remembered it, but Spoleto was the town which really enchanted him in Umbria, as he claimed it was "[his] most wonderful discovery in Italy. There is such an incredible wealth of virtually unknown beauty, there are mountains, valleys, bridges, oak forests, monasteries, and waterfalls!" Spoleto is indeed rich in interest, both geographical and artistic. Different styles coexist peacefully in apparent disorder, bearing witness to the city's traditional wealth, the origins of which are lost in time. Spoleto, along with all its other arts, has a famous theatrical tradition which continues today with the Festival of the Two Worlds. A regular international fixture, the festival concentrates the best and the newest productions of drama, opera, dance, and music into two busy weeks. For once, the lure of what is ancient, which can be a little overwhelming for all its wonder, gives way to the inventions of the modern, avant-garde world.

The center of Todi, a long, rectangular piazza on the hill above the Tiber valley, perfectly recreates the atmosphere of the town which ruled Amelia and Terni. At one corner of this majestic rectangle, at the top of a flight of stairs, stands the Duomo. Opposite stands the Palace of the Priors with its crenellated walls and imperious five-sided tower. Along one of the long sides stand the Palaces of the People and of the Captain, joined by a wide external staircase. Lying between them and the Palace of the Priors is Piazza Garibaldi, which forms a kind of balcony overlooking the valley and the river Tiber.

Alone, in the middle of a vast green lawn and visible from afar to anyone approaching from either Terni or Orvieto, stands the Church of St. Mary of the Consolation. Built around a central plan and likened to "an immense and incomparable ostensory," it is possibly the work of Bramante. It is an unusual sight compared with the familiar Umbria of contemplative Romanesque architecture, locked inside its own walls. Here the space is open to the valley and the circularity of the plan evokes the perfection of a divine design. Physically, the

60 bottom The little Porziuncola Chapel (which literally means "small piece of ground") is, perhaps, the place most reminiscent of St. Francis. It was here that he founded his Order, that he met St. Clare, and that he died in 1226. The building consists of just one room, with a pointed barrel-vault ceiling.

61 The interior of the Benedictine Church of St. Peter, built in the second half of the thirteenth century, is lit almost entirely by the light from the central rose window in the façade. The beamed ceiling is supported by closely-set ranks of large ogival arches.

building's powerful appearance provides a sample of the magniloquence of the Baroque style yet to come.

Orvieto looks like an island above the wide Perugian valley. Built on a rocky platform, well-protected and easily defendable, it was always an obvious choice for its peoples and its sovereigns, including Etruscans, Romans, Goths, Byzantines, Lombards, and the massive presence of the Papal court. It was at Orvieto that Pope Innocent III proclaimed the Fourth Crusade, Pope Martin IV was elected in the presence of Charles of Anjou, and Louis of France was canonized in the presence of Pope Boniface VIII. More than any other Umbrian city, Orvieto is identified with its grandiose cathedral. Its magnificent position makes it the obvious point of reference for both religious and secular events in the town. The church is similar in style to the French model, where Gothic architecture had already developed. Its deep portals, pinnacled pediments, and glorious carved rose window create a façade which is a miracle of harmony, equilibrium, and precious decoration.

62-63 A sky lit by the moon and filled with stars makes a calm and sober backdrop to the dramatic foreground scene of the Capture of Christ. The fresco, attributed to Giotto's great Sienese pupil Pietro Lorenzetti, is in the left transept of the Lower Church at Assisi and dates from 1326-29.

Perugia: by ancient stairways among monuments of art and architecture

64 top The Maggiore Fountain, Perugia's most famous medieval fountain, dominates Piazza dei Priori, nowadays called Piazza IV Novembre. A late thirteenth-century inscription bears the names of its architect Fra Bevignate and of Nicola and Giovanni Pisano, who sculpted the marble statues and reliefs which decorate the two polygonal basins.

64 bottom A simple and austere church, also known as "Sant'Agnolo," St. Michael Archangel is a paleo-Christian rotunda dating from the fifth and sixth centuries. The tambour of the rotunda has triple sets of windows facing in the directions of the four cardinal points and of the four arms of a cross.

64-65 With their powerful buttresses, the façade and the outside walls of St. Dominic (dating from the end of the fourteenth and the beginning of the fifteenth centuries) have retained the look of Cistercian architecture and of the Dominican Church of Santa Maria Novella. The church was taken as the model for the Duomo of Perugia.

65 bottom St. Peter's Tower
of the Benedictine
monastery of the same name
is both a bell tower and a
lookout. Reliable sources
record that its foundations
stand over an Etruscan
tomb. The twelve-sided part
dates from the thirteenth
century and the cornice,
supported by a ring of
brackets, was originally
designed to be a walkway.

66-67 The old city is criss-crossed by these characteristic steep lanes, lined with stone or brick, sometimes narrow and twisting, with arches which suddenly open up onto the countryside or an old palace. The Middle Ages have left important remains in this city, which have been preserved thanks to the intelligence and respect of its inhabitants.

68-69 The last light of day leaves the rooftops of Perugia while artificial lights start to appear in the streets and houses. Night is ready to embrace the entire city and conceal its different spirits: Etruscan, Roman, medieval, and papal. Perugia is about to be wrapped in dusk's dark mantle.

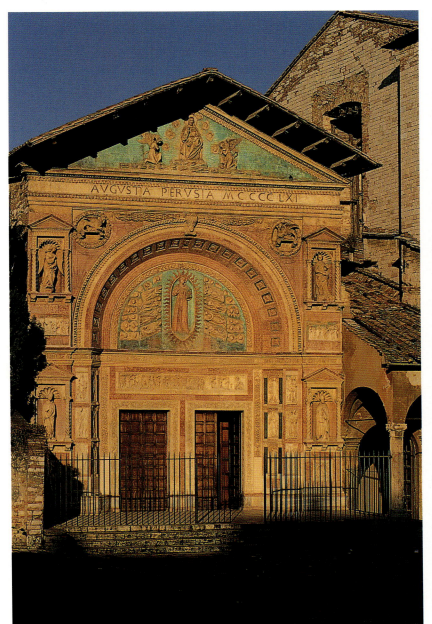

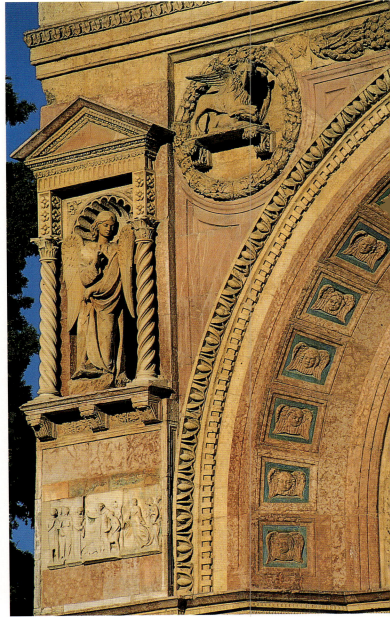

70-71 The fine Renaissance architecture of St. Bernadine's Oratory in Perugia, built in 1457, is a splendid setting for its richly decorated façade, the work of Donatello's Florentine pupil Agostino di Duccio. In the tympanum, Christ is surrounded by angels and cherubs as He blesses the world. The lunette contains Saint Bernadine of Siena in the flaming almond, surrounded by angel and cherub musicians. The canopied niche on the left of the lunette shows the Angel of the Annunciation. The soft, wavy lines of the clothes worn by the artist's subjects are characteristic of his style, giving them a unique appearance of lightness.

72 *The noble Collegio del Cambio (Exchange Guild) in Perugia. The photograph shows the Audience Room which was designed for important civic functions of government, charity, and justice. Towards the end of the fifteenth Century the Consuls who met there commissioned their fellow citizen Perugino to fresco the Audience Room in a way suited to its use for public meetings and the administration of justice, with figures of the Prophets and the Sybils, and the cardinal virtues and the figures which best represented them in ancient times. The wooden paneling on the walls also dates from the last decade of the fifteenth century.*

73 *Not everyone agrees with the attribution of this splendid altarpiece of the Adoration of the Magi (1476-78), kept in the National Gallery of Perugia, to Perugino, but it demonstrates all the ingredients typical of his style: warm, mellow colors (the painting is traditionally considered the earliest oil painting in Umbria); a taste for costume and detailed physiognomy; immense serenity, grace, and elegance; and the vastness of the landscape's horizon. The youth who looks out from the painting on the far left is the artist himself, Pietro Vannucci, known as Perugino.*

74-75 *In 1582 the Hall of the Notaries, originally the seat of public meetings inside the Priors' Palace, became the Salone dell'Arte dei Notai (Art Salon of the Notaries). The ceiling with its eight massive arches, the walls, and the window jambs were frescoed by the Roman artists working on the Upper Church at Assisi.*

ASSISI:
THE STRENGTH OF
THE SPIRIT

76-77 The Duomo of Assisi, dating from the twelfth century and dedicated to Saint Rufino, has one of the richest and most eloquent sculpture bestiaries in Italian Romanesque architecture. Griffins, monsters, and devilish reptiles alternate with portrayals of biblical scenes and the symbols of the Evangelists which surround the central rose window. The lunette over the main door contains a sculpted Christ of majestic and awesome holiness.

78-79 A charming nighttime view of the Piazza del Comune at Assisi with lights reflecting on the fourteenth-century Palace of the Priors and the Tower of the People, which was begun in 1212.

80-81 The town of Assisi sits on hilly terrain. The imposing outline of the Sacred Convent of St. Francis is immediately visible from this angle, looking more like a powerful bastion than a religious building.

82-83 There is a large open area in front of the façade of the Upper Church of St. Francis. Work started on the building on July 17, 1228, the day after the saint was canonized.

84 The photograph illustrates the grandiosity and richly-detailed decoration of the Lower Church's central nave. Built immediately after the death of the saint by order of Brother Elia, the vicar-general of the Franciscans, the building is composed of two superimposed churches. Both churches were frescoed by the greatest artists of the time, Cimabue and Giotto. The walls of the Lower Church bear masterpieces by Pietro Lorenzetti and Simone Martini.

85 The cross-vault of the first span of the Upper Church. The frescoes of the four Doctors of the Church, Saint Jerome, Saint Augustine, Saint Gregory, and Saint Ambrose, are attributed to the young Giotto and date from 1293.

87 top The left transept of the Lower Church houses this masterpiece painted by Pietro Lorenzetti and a few helpers in the second decade of the fourteenth century. The subject is the Passion of Christ. The detail of the barrel vault with **The Entry into Jerusalem** *exhibits unusual importance given to the architecture and uses particularly rich and vital colors.*

87 bottom The unmistakable style of Simone Martini is evident in the elegance of these two court musicians with their multi-colored clothes, and the dreamlike air which accompanies this ceremony of the Investiture of St. Martin in the eponymous chapel, in the Lower Church of St. Francis at Assisi (1317).

86-87 The fact that the lower church-crypt acts as a foundation for the construction above is clearly visible in the squat proportions of its wide cross-vaults set on full arches and supported by massive, low, pillars. The single nave model found at Assisi was particularly suited to preaching and the viewing of the frescoes on the walls.

NORCIA: THE UNSPOILED CHARM OF THE SMALLER TOWNS

88-89 *Roman Nursia, the modern Norcia, was the birthplace in A.D. 480 of Saint Benedict and his twin sister Saint Scolastica. According to tradition, the cathedral is built above the house where the two saints were born. The present building dates from the end of the fourteenth century. The handsome Gothic portal and the rose window are adorned by the statues of the two saints in their niches. The monument to Saint Benedict in front of the church dates from 1880.*

90 top This lunette with the Virgin and Child, flanked at the sides by the twin saints Saint Benedict and Saint Scolastica, is found on the façade of St. Augustine's.

90 bottom Another lunette, this time on the main door of St. Benedict's, with the Virgin and Child between kneeling angels.

91 Little known to the wider public, the Church of St. Augustine contains some precious and rare surprises, such as this powerful late-fifteenth-century fresco with the figure of the saint.

92-93 The heart of the little town of Norcia is in Piazza San Benedetto. The saint's statue is surrounded by the town's main buildings: the Palazzo Comunale, the Church of St. Benedict (both of which can be seen in the photograph), the Castellina Fort, and the Duomo.

Montefalco:
TRIUMPHANT AMID
BANNERS AND KNIGHTS

QVANDO · B̄ · F · PREDICAVIT · AVIBVS · APVD · MEVANEVM · DEMV̄ · BENEDIXIT · MŌTEM · FALCONĒ · ET · P̄PLV̄S ·

94 In these fifteenth-century frescoes by Benozzo Gozzoli, the real protagonists are the elegant citizens of the period, the taste for ornament, and the courtly ideal. In the artist's opinion, figures had the same importance as architecture and landscape. The picture shows the Blessing of the Consuls of Bevagna and Montefalco with Gozzoli's client, Fra Jacopo da Montefalco, kneeling on the right.

95 The central apse of the ex-church of Saint Francis at Montefalco -- nowadays the building is an art gallery -- is a masterpiece by Benozzo Gozzoli. After leaving his teacher, Beato Angelico, he took on this large independent commission of the Chronicles of Saint Francis.

SPOLETO: THE COLORS OF TOWN AND COUNTRY

96 *The private chapel of Bishop Costantino Eroli in the Duomo of Spoleto is adorned with a majestic Virgin on athrone with the Child and Saints John the Baptist and Stephen. Above her is the Eternal Father in glory, surrounded by angels and cherubs. The work, dated 1497, is attributed to Pinturicchio, one of Perugino's most prolific pupils.*

97 *The Romanesque Duomo of Spoleto, dedicated to Our Lady of the Assumption, was begun after the city was destroyed by Frederick Barbarossa in 1155. The rose window is particularly worthy of note as well as the bell tower, mentioned in the oldest records as a defensive tower, the mosaic with Christ enthroned between Saints Mary and John, dated 1207, and the portico, which was added at the end of the fifteenth century.*

98-99 *The Duomo of Spoleto. The frescoes in the bowl-shaped vault of the apse are the work of another outstanding fifteenth-century artist, Filippo Lippi. The scene of the Coronation of the Virgin is the last work completed by the artist, who died in 1469.*

100-101 *This view shows the unique beauty of Piazza del Duomo at Spoleto, one of the most charming squares in Italy. The contrast of the colors is stunning: the white of the paving stones, the warm colors of the houses, the pink patina of the Duomo with the bright gold of its mosaic, and the green of the hills in the background.*

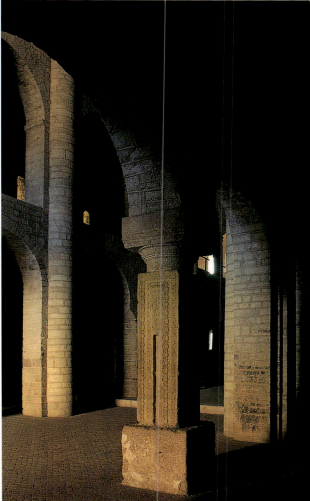

102-103 The austerely Romanesque church of St. Euphemia at Spoleto dates from the twelfth century. The bare, three-naved structure with its women's galleries automatically encourages silence and prayer. For a long time the church was dedicated to Saint Lucia, who is commemorated in a fresco of 1455 on the round pillar of the second span.

104-105 The Gattaponi Bridge is a symbol of Spoleto. Named after its designer, Matteo Gattaponi da Gubbio, it is a footbridge and an aqueduct, and was built in the fourteenth century in local limestone, probably on an existing Roman structure. It is 755 feet long and crosses the ravine beneath it with ten spectacularly tall arches.

Todi: AUSTERITY AND FIGHTING SPIRIT

106 top A view of Todi, a medieval town with ancient roots, on its steep hill above the Tiber Valley.

106 bottom The sanctuary of the Virgin of the Consolation at Todi has a curious clover-leaf design. The building consists of a central cube topped by a high cupola with a four-apsed tambour, one circular and the others polygonal. It is one of the rare sixteenth-century churches in Umbria, and many famous architects were involved in building it, from Peruzzi to Sangallo the Younger, Vignola, and Alessi.

107 The thirteenth-century crenellated Palace of the People and, further back, the Palace of the Captain with its beautiful triple Gothic windows. Joined by a large external staircase, they are what gives the Piazza del Popolo at Todi its austere character. The Romanesque Duomo sits at one end of the long, rectangular square at the top of a flight of steps.

108 Located at the highest point of the town's hill within the circle of the oldest set of walls, building began on the Franciscan church of Todi's patron Saint, Fortunato, in 1292. Work on this delightful building continued until the second half of the fifteenth century.

109 left Only the lower part of the façade of the Church of St. Fortunato is decorated, in the style of Jacopo della Quercia. It bears some similarity to the façade of the Duomo of Orvieto which was done a century earlier.

109 right From inside, the size of the church is revealed. It is a large and airy three-naved building, whose splendid, tall cross-vaults give it an air of solemn majesty.

ORVIETO: HOW TO EMBROIDER WITH ARCHITECTURE

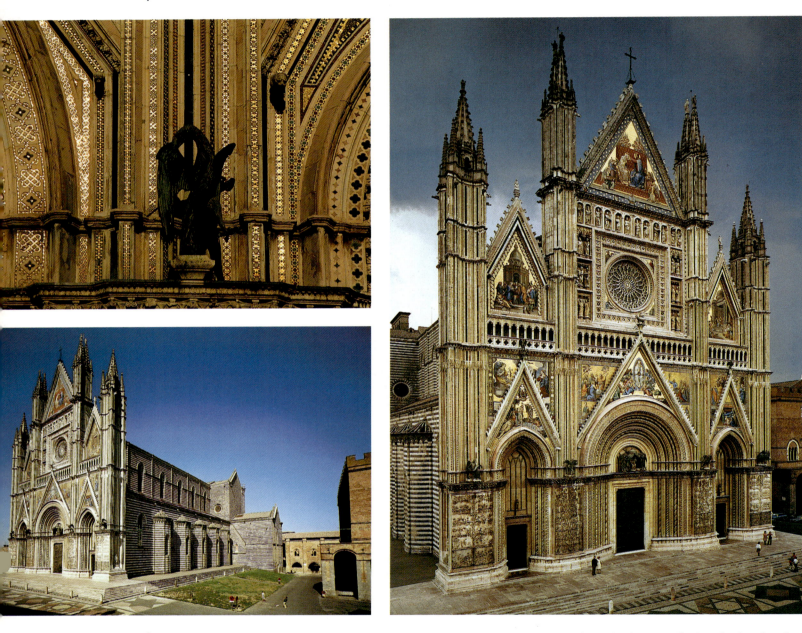

110-111 The Duomo of Orvieto is the true symbol of this Umbrian town as well as one of the greatest works of Gothic architecture in Italy. In fact, its illustrated front wall has been compared to a polyptychal Gothic altar frontal. Building began on the Duomo in 1290 in commemoration of the miracle of Bolsena, and was intended as an authentic Romanesque building, albeit one of exceptional height and width. Around 1310, Lorenzo Maitani of Siena was commissioned to continue the work in line with contemporary modern criteria which produced the exceptional carved and painted decoration of the façade and the chancel. The greater part of the façade is bas-relief, mosaic, and gold, and produces a pictorial effect which emphasizes the image of the church triumphant. In addition, the molded buttresses surmounted by tall pinnacles, the pointed recesses above the doors and crowning the naves, and the galleries of pointed arches only increase the fascinating, unique appearance of this architectural masterpiece. The beautiful rose window, set in its square frame, deserves separate mention. Completed in 1359, it is attributed to the great Florentine sculptor, Andrea Orcagna.

GLORIOSVS·APOSTOLORVM·CHORVS·

112-113 The Chapel of St. Brizio, inside the Duomo of Orvieto, houses the celebrated cycle of frescoes by Luca Signorelli who Vasari defined as "dexterous" in drawing and "agile" in his use of color. The Last Judgement is, in the words of Vasari, "a very, very, beautiful piece of work, bizarre and whimsical for the variety of seeing so many angels, demons, earthquakes, fires, ruins, and a great many of the miracles of the Antichrist." The picture on the left is a scene portraying the Summoning of the Elect to Heaven. On the right is the scene from the end of the world, The Damned in Hell. The Last Judgement, the Sermon of the Antichrist, The End of the World: these are the Apocalyptical themes which, from 1499 onwards, Signorelli dealt with in his best work, leaving them behind as a kind of testament. His frescoes are a tremendously effective portrayal of the torment of conscience which affected the mentality and the collective imagination of society at the end of the fifteenth century, prey to catastrophic foretellings, horoscopes, and terrifying predictions, not to mention Savonarola's fire-and-brimstone preaching.

114-115 St. Patrick's Well was built by order of Pope Clement VII while he was in Orvieto during the Sack of Rome in 1527. The well was intended to supply the town with drinking water in the event of a siege. The complex design is attributed to Antonio da Sangallo the Younger and comprises a cylinder which is 203 feet deep and 43 wide, around which two superimposed, independent flights of stairs wind, one for the descent and one for the ascent, each reaching right to the bottom of the well. Leonardo da Vinci had designed a similar system of stairs for a brothel.

115 top The serious, imposing air of the thirteenth-century Palace of the People at Orvieto is lightened somewhat by the elegant three-light windows of the huge hall on the first floor.

115 bottom The Hotel Badia near Orvieto is an example of intelligent re-use in respect of the old traditions. The building was originally a thirteenth century abbey but has been converted into a hotel.

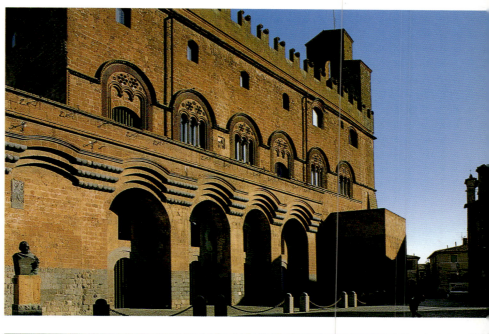

116-117 This panorama of Orvieto shows the dangerous position the town occupies on the top of a large outcrop of tuff in the valley of Paglia.

118-119 The Palace of the Consuls at Gubbio is architecturally one of the most important municipal buildings of the Middle Ages. This extraordinary undertaking required the construction of huge supporting foundations, some two stories high, on the slopes of Gubbio's mountain. The foundations do not only support the palace itself but the square too, which is nothing more than a huge hanging terrace. It is not known with certainty who the architect was, but many think that it was the work of a youthful Matteo Gattaponi, the designer of the bridge at Spoleto which bears his name.

GUBBIO: IN DEFIANCE OF CLIFFS AND CRAGS

119 left The richly decorated chancel in St. Augustine's church at Gubbio contains fresco cycles illustrating the lives of the saint, the four Evangelists, and the Last Judgment. The work is attributed to Ottaviano Nelli and his workshop, and dates from the second decade of the fifteenth century.

119 right The photograph captures a charming view of the center of old Gubbio. Prototype of the medieval town, Gubbio still has many historic buildings within its characteristic layout. Encircling walls shelter the township and the Cathedral and Ducal Palace are situated so as to dominate all the other buildings.

120-121 A detail of the entrance to the Palace of the Consuls from what used to be the ancient Iguvium. Today the city art gallery is housed inside the palace and is well worth an extended visit.

FOLIGNO: LORDLY HONOR AND COURTESY

123 The Hall of Stars in the Trinci Palace in Foligno is like an Academy. The walls are decorated with frescoes by an unknown hand, portraying all the liberal arts: Grammar, Dialectics, Music (seen here), Geometry, Philosophy, Astrology, Arithmetic, and Rhetoric.

122 left The photograph shows part of the façade of San Feliciano, the Duomo of Foligno, which records show to have been completed in 1113 and frequently modified over the years. The church gives onto Piazza della Repubblica in the center of the town.

122 top right The courtly frescoes which adorn the noble Trinci Palace, residence of the lords of Foligno, date from the second decade of the fifteenth century. The codes of good breeding and of chivalry seem to be the only worries of the two gallants with the bright clothes.

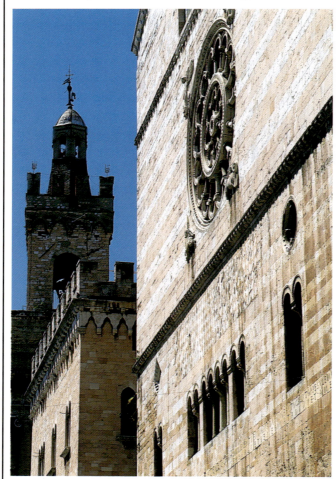

122 bottom right
The unknown painter of this rich secular cycle dating from the beginning of the fifteenth century reveals his education in the Humanities in the Hall of Stars in the Trinci Palace, where he has portrayed the liberal arts: the photograph is of his portrait of Grammar.

SPELLO:
BREATHING THE AIR OF ANCIENT TIMES THROUGH THE LANES AND AMONG THE HOUSES

124 One of the characteristic narrow, uphill, streets of Spello, Via Arco di Augusto. The Roman town Hispellum can be seen in the walls and arches which were incorporated into other buildings in successive ages, all testifying to the town's long history.

125 The stone houses and brick-and-cobble streets of the medieval period have been preserved unchanged, giving Spello its unique and unmistakable air.

126-127 The unreal light of a gathering storm bathes the houses in the town of Spello, which dominates the surrounding countryside.

128-129 Ranks of angel musicians painted by Giotto and his assistants frame the Triumph of Saint Francis *on the ceiling of the Lower Church.*

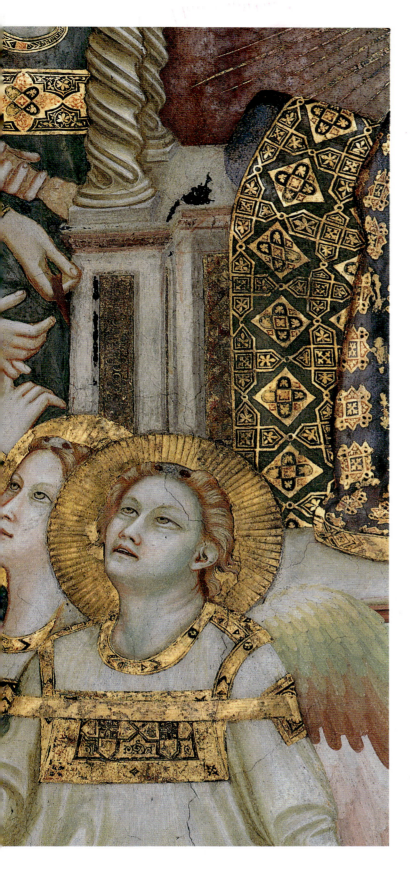

THE MYSTICISM
OF NATURE

The famous monk of Assisi, mystical, revolutionary, and modern, and his **Canticle of the Sun** today represent an ecological code of behavior and of choices. The direction which Saint Francis pointed out eight centuries ago, towards cosmic fraternization and respect for nature, is the one we now know to be indispensable for the survival of our planet. The picture of the poor, humble saint who married Lady Poverty and kissed lepers, always ready to sacrifice himself, guided by his love for his neighbors and for all creatures, has undergone a considerable evolution over time. Increasingly, Francis appears as a man who was both fascinating and awkward, pacifist and revolutionary, enchanted by the beauty of creation but not enough to lose sight of its concreteness, its history, and social reality. A man of radical and determined choices, he offered new values in contrast to the ones emerging at the time with the birth of the merchant class. There is no doubt that Francis was a child of his time, the Middle Ages, but today his teachings have an extraordinarily modern appeal to us, an example of rebellion against the uniquely Christian arrogance by which the Bible placed man at the center of the world, in a position to dominate it.

Francis challenged the Biblical picture of Adam in the Garden of Eden, described in **Genesis** as the keeper of all creatures, free to dominate, manipulate, and exploit nature to the point of destroying it. His own example was rather of responsibility towards and respect for nature. His way was not to dominate it, but to find signs of the God in which he believed in the whole of creation: in water, in the sun, in the moon, in fire, in the song of the crickets, and in everything. His universal brotherhood is none other than the much-invoked new alliance between man and nature. In the face of the merchants and the usurers of the thirteenth century among whom he lived, Francis preached being and not having, respect and not dominion, quality and not quantity. His was the new world in which the church bells were being joined by the clocks of the civic towers, in which the epoch of a Church consisting of sext and nones was giving way to the epoch of the merchant and making money.

130 *Giotto's masterpiece of 1296-1300, the* Miracle of the Spring, *can be admired inside the Upper Church. Saint Francis is accompanied on a journey to a hermitage by a peasant, who is exhausted by thirst. The saint kneels down,* raises his hands to heaven, and prays until he is answered. The thirsty man drinks the water which gushes from the rock in answer to Francis's prayer. Giotto added two monks to the scene, as witnesses to the miracle.

131 *This fresco in the Upper Church portraying the saint* Preaching to the Birds *is also by Giotto. Close to the village of Bevagna Saint Francis saw a great flock of birds and, according to the* Legenda Maior, *greeted them as if* they were intelligent creatures and blessed them with the sign of the cross, at which the birds showed their joy in a marvelous way. Giotto's portrayal of nature in this fresco demonstrates tremendous wealth of detail.

Today, on the other hand, the concepts of development and progress based solely on income, and the idea of what comprises well-being and quality of life, are being questioned, while Francis, who believed that the environment belonged to all and to everyone, who bridges generations and places limits on economic growth and the exploitation of resources, is being rediscovered and newly appreciated. The influence of Francis and of Franciscanism has been essential in Umbria, not only from a religious point of view, but also for its art and civil history. The land of saints but also the cradle of "improving" movements which many considered heretical, before Francis Umbria was for a long period the stage for burgeoning revolution. The Flagellants, who paraded through towns behind cross-bearing priests, striking and whipping themselves and crying out, the Cathars, the Paterines, the Little Brothers, and numerous sects thrived during this era. Franciscanism served to repair all the fractures in society. It was a grandiose movement which the other great orders, Augustine and Benedictine, were able to live with. It was a mighty spur for construction in the material sense as well. Churches and monasteries, painters and artists were mobilized on the wave of the great fervor, aroused by the mendicant orders in particular. Their great solidity was based on ancient roots, in the convents and hermitages which arose at Monteluco, Ferentillo, Norcia, and on Mt. Subasio. The monasteries were the outposts for new towns which were growing larger. Always built on the outskirts of the towns, they contributed to starting a process of renewed urban growth and were eventually incorporated within the new city walls. Although it is true that Francis was the most charismatic among the figures who left their mark on the region's history, there were other, equally important, names which cannot be ignored such as Saint Benedict of Norcia, the great architect of monasterial religiosity and activism, supporter of the Catholic edifice during its earliest and harshest centuries, and founder of monasteries which were essential to the history of Western culture, as well as his twin sister Saint Scolastica. Saint Clare of Assisi also followed the example of Francis by giving up her wealth and founding the Poor Clares, as did Saint Rita of Cascia. Today, the echo of popular devotion

132 The Upper Church of St. Francis at Assisi, pictured here, dates from the middle of the thirteenth century. Work started on the site two years before the saint's death in 1226 and it immediately became the hub of the Franciscan movement. The building consists of two churches placed one above the other. The lower of the two contains the tomb of the Order's founder and became a place of pilgrimage and of popular religious observance immediately, while the upper church is intended for preaching, a central activity in the Franciscan doctrine and for all the mendicant orders. The two churches both have single-nave layouts with a transept and an apse, supported outside the walls by long cylindrical buttresses on top and massive arches below.

133 Pietro Lorenzetti's fresco of Christ Entering Jerusalem, in the left-hand transept of the Lower Church at Assisi. Followed by the Apostles, Jesus is acclaimed in great triumph. In the background two youths pick olive branches to celebrate the arrival of the Messiah. The work contains proof of a detailed study of space, emphasized by its pure, shining use of colors.

can still be heard in the numerous religious festivals: Corpus Domini at Orvieto, the celebration of Saint Rita at Cascia, the Elevation of the Ceri at Gubbio, and the Flower Ceremony at Spello.

The religious spirit is undoubtedly one of the characteristic features of this region and it can be seen too in the earthly lives of other Umbrians who have passed into history. One example is Celestine V, Boniface VIII's predecessor, who was stigmatized by Dante in **The Inferno** for "his cowardly refusal." However, the figure who left behind the strongest mystical testimony is the solitary, fascinating figure of Jacopone da Todi. In his **Lauds**, out of an almost excessive love for God, he invokes every kind of evil, every dissolution of the flesh, every curse and terror in a fury of self-abasement worthy of the apocalyptic images painted by Signorelli at Orvieto.

The mystery of the monastic life and the evocative power of the silent monasteries and their cloisters lives on as part of the traditional Umbrian rite of hospitality. The Benedictine monastery of St. Mary of the Mount at Bevagna welcomes people, individually or in groups, on the condition that they respect the strict rhythms of the cloistered life. Loggias and stairs connect the different buildings which surround the internal garden, a true **hortus conclusus** where prayers and meditation are encouraged. There is a more prosaic element, too. The monastic community is famous for its products including honey, jams, grappa, oil, and sweets, all of which are served to guests. The ancient convent of St. Magno at Amelia offers the same kind of hospitality, where the Benedictine nuns have lived since the thirteenth century. An exquisitely Umbrian veneration and respect can be seen here in the way that the region's monumental trees are looked after and protected. Legend has it that Saint Bernadine's linden tree (52 feet high with a girth of almost 20 feet) was planted by the inhabitants of Todi in 1426 in memory of the saint's preaching. At Narni, there is Saint Speco's chestnut tree. The holly oak of the Carceri Hermitage stands at Assisi. The public gardens of Umbria represent yet another example of the Umbrians' respect for the environment, recognizing the riches over which they have the good fortune to stand guard.

134-135 The allegories of the three virtues, Poverty, Chastity, and Obedience, together with the **Triumph of Saint Francis**, are all in the vaulted cells of the Lower Church and are the work of Giotto and his school.

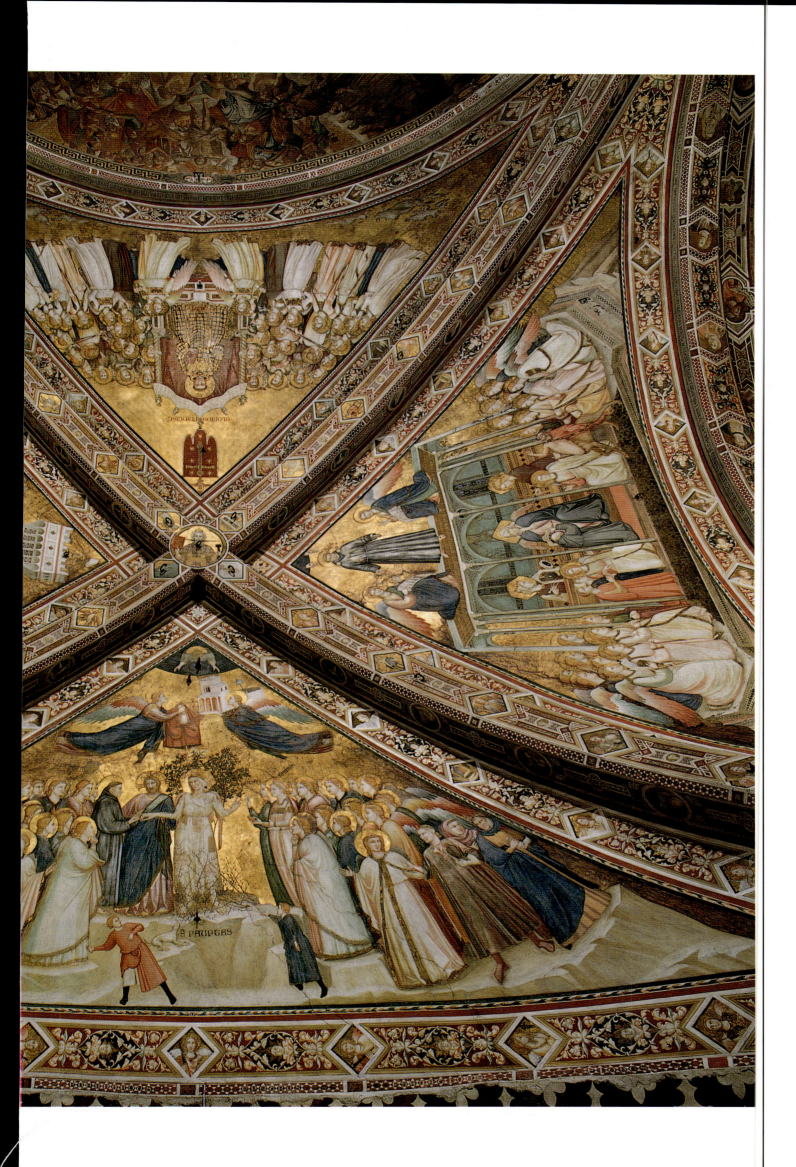

137 Giotto's fresco in the Upper Church depicting Saint Francis in the Confirmation of the Rule. *The maestro shows his deepening investigation of the relationship between figures and their background, a relationship he never left to chance.*

The boldly foreshortened interior is used as a frame to gather the three groups of figures within the wall's three arches. From left to right they are: the brothers, Saint Francis in the center, and Pope Innocent III, surrounded by high prelates, as he blesses the saint.

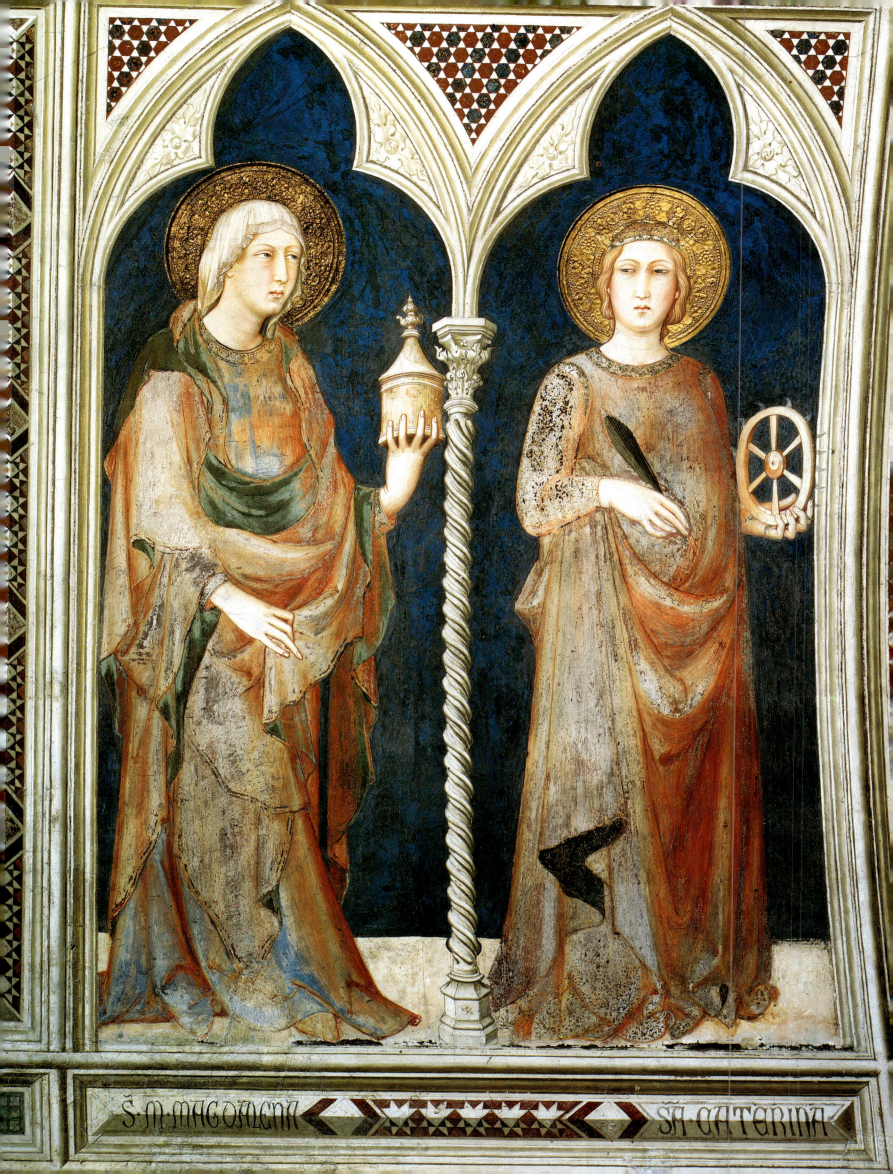

S. M. MAGOMENA · SŃ CATARINA

140-141 *In this work portraying Saint Clare, a disciple of Saint Francis and foundress of the Order of the Poor Clares, her face has the holiness of a Byzantine icon. This precious portrait can be admired at Assisi, in the right-hand transept of the church dedicated to the saint. It is the work of an unknown master of Cimabue's circle.*

141 top *In this view of Assisi the Church of St. Clare seems to dominate the surrounding countryside. Its Gothic construction is similar to the structure of the Upper Church of St. Francis, who was Saint Clare's companion in faith, although the use of white and pink limestone in alternate stripes gives the building a quite unique and unusual character.*

141 bottom *The Church of St. Clare, built between 1257 and 1265, contains some valuable painting masterpieces. The vaults of the apse bear the figures of saints, probably dating from the first half of the thirteenth century.*

142-143 *The first rays of evening light up Assisi in all its uniqueness: faith, art, and history meet and entwine in this ancient city.*

144 *One of the two entrances to Perugia's twelfth-century Palaca of the Priors is guarded by a stone statue of a griffin clawing a bull.*

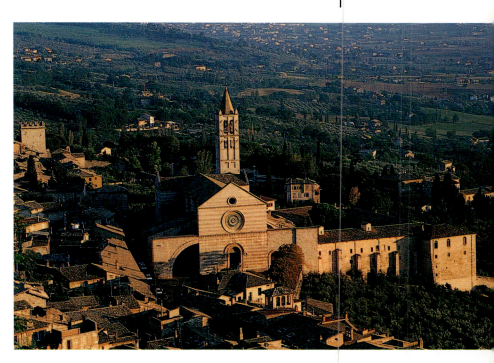